Shelly Bean the Sports Queen

Plays a game of Catch

09

By Shelly Boyum-Breen

Illustrated by Marieka Heinlen

DEDICATION: This book belongs to all young sports fans that love to play, work hard, try new things, and dream big. When I was six, I dreamed of playing in the NBA, NHL, NFL and MLB. I worked hard to make my dreams come true, and I made many friends and memories along the way. While I did not end up playing professional sports, I did do a lot of other cool things with my life—like write these books for kids! I am active every day and eager to share my passion for playing sports with others. My hope is that Shelly Bean inspires YOU to play.

ACKNOWLEDGEMENTS: A special thank-you to my youth coaches, parents, brothers, spouse, children, nephews and nieces and many friends who have supported me as I've grown as an athlete and as the creator of Shelly Bean the Sports Queen. Finally, an enormous "thank you" to the "backers" and Team Bean who worked creatively as a unit to help bring Shelly Bean to life.

PUBLISHED BY:
Level Field Press, LLC
2960 Everest Lane
Plymouth, MN 55447
shellybeanthesportsqueen.com

Illustrated By: Marieka Meinlen
Design & Print Production:
Blue Tricycle, Inc.

Boyum-Breen, Shelly.
    Shelly Bean the Sports Queen plays a game of catch /
by Shelly Boyum-Breen ; illustrated by Marieka Heinlen.
    pages cm
    SUMMARY: Shelly Bean the Sports Queen learns about friendship and team spirit while playing baseball and softball.
    Audience: Grade 2.
    ISBN 978-1-4951-1494-6

    1. Baseball--Juvenile fiction. 2. Softball--Juvenile fiction. 3. Sports for girls--Juvenile fiction.
4. Team sports--Juvenile fiction. [1. Baseball--Fiction.
2. Softball--Fiction. 3. Sports for girls--Fiction.
4. Team sports--Fiction. 5. Friendship--Fiction.]
I. Heinlen, Marieka, illustrator. II. Title.

PZ7.B6972Shp 2014   [E]
                  QBI14-600108

Team Shelly Bean

Shelly Bean loves to try new sports and she wants you to try new sports too! Let's see what she learns to play today. Then follow the tips at the end of the book and start playing with her!

Spike
co-mascot

Shelly Bean
the sports Queen

Buster
co-mascot

Ben
bigger brother

Matt
big brother

Maya
best buddy

It was a hot summer day when Shelly Bean and her brothers, Ben and Matt, went to watch their cousin Olivia at her softball game. It was so fun to see a lot of neighbors and classmates at the ballpark.

Shelly Bean spotted her fiends Maya and Audrey in the stands. They were having a great time cheering, eating popcorn and singing with the crowd.

Take me out to the ball game...

Shelly Bean was so excited she held her breath when Olivia was up to bat. She loved watching the runners and the sound of the ball hitting the bat. Crack!

Shelly Bean couldn't believe how easily the players could catch and throw. She wanted to try it, too!

After the game, some players stayed to play catch. Olivia asked Shelly Bean and her brothers to join them.

WATCH FOR FOUL BALLS

Shelly Bean hadn't used a mitt before, so Coach Carol gave her one that fit her hand. Olivia asked Shelly Bean to be her partner.

9

Olivia was really good at softball. As Shelly Bean tossed the ball underhand she felt butterflies in her stomach. It popped up high in the air—but Olivia caught it!

Make sure your glove is up and ready to catch the ball.

Then, Olivia tossed the ball back to Shelly Bean underhand. She watched the ball, raised her hands above her face, and felt the ball land with a thud in the pocket of her mitt.

Olivia and Shelly Bean practiced throwing underhand and catching. "Let's go for three times without dropping it. One! Two!" Shelly Bean was really getting the hang of it. Swoop. Pop! Thud. Suddenly, they got three in a row!

1, 2, 3!

WE DID IT!

Shelly Bean started to throw the ball to Olivia again. This time, Spike wanted to join the fun. He jumped up and caught the ball in his mouth and started running. Hey!

The kids all laughed as Spike brought the ball back to Shelly Bean and she patted him on the back.

"Now let's try overhand!" said Olivia. "Uh, ok," said Shelly Bean nervously.

Shelly Bean's first toss didn't go very far, and bounced through the grass to Olivia's feet. "Hmmm," Shelly thought. "Maybe this isn't so easy after all."

She saw the others out of the corner of her eye playing catch. They were throwing the ball so hard to each other it would smack in the mitts!

Shelly Bean decided to ask Coach Carol for some tips.

Coach Carol was happy to help, "Reach your throwing arm back behind your head and twist your body. When you let go of the ball, follow-through by reaching toward Olivia."

Shelly Bean tried a few more times. Smack! Finally, the ball made it into Olivia's mitt. "Gosh Spike, throwing and catching overhand is a lot harder to learn!" said Shelly Bean.

"May I please come back again after your game and try throwing overhand a few more times?" asked Shelly Bean. "I think I need more practice."

"Of course little cousin," said Olivia "I'm so proud of you. Maybe next time you can bat and run the bases. I think Spike might even run with you!"

Shelly Bean, her brothers, and Spike left the park and walked back home before it got dark. It was time for dinner with the family and they had a lot of news to share.

Shelly Bean was pretty tired from her busy day, but there was one more thing she was excited to do. Shelly and Spike did their extra big super dive onto her bed and she pulled out her art supplies and her special crown of sports.

Shelly Bean finished her baseball mitt charm and said, "We did it again, Spike!" She put her colorful crown on her head, looked in her mirror and smiled her big smile.

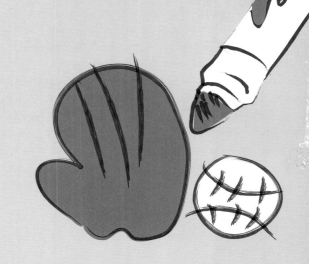

I am Shelly Bean the Sports Queen!

She was proud of herself. Today, Shelly learned how to play catch.

TIPS

Tips for Playing Catch

Try using a soft ball instead of a baseball when beginning to avoid injury. These tips are made for a right-handed thrower. Left-handers should simply reverse hands.

Throwing (overhand):

1. Hold the ball in your right hand with your three middle fingers on the top of the ball and your thumb and pinky on each side of the ball.

2. Turn your body so that your left foot and your left arm point to your target or the person you are throwing to. Bring the ball back behind your head with your right hand. The ball should be above your right shoulder.

Sometimes it helps to think of your body making the shape of the letter "T" with your elbows and shoulders up.

3. Rotate your body towards your target. Release the ball towards your target as your arm is nearly fully extended.

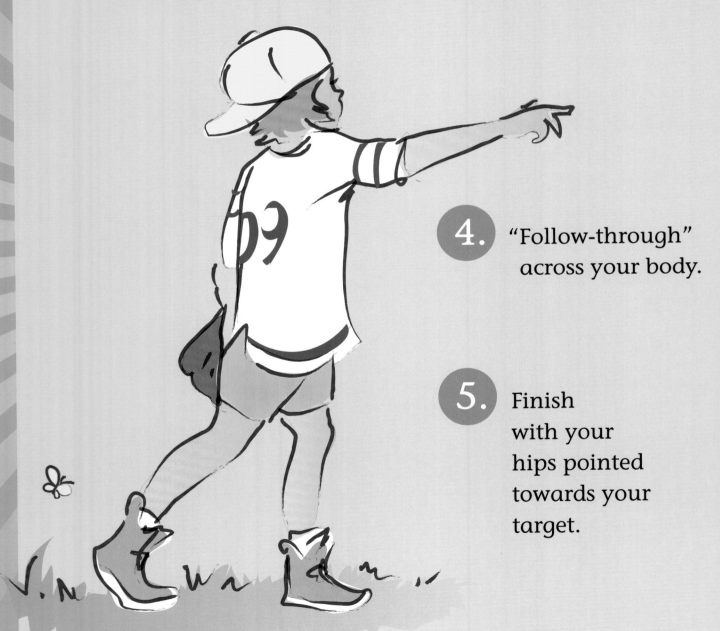

4. "Follow-through" across your body.

5. Finish with your hips pointed towards your target.

Catching:

1. Keep your eyes on the ball! Watch the ball leave your partner's hand until it is in your hands.

2. With your mitt on your left hand, spread your left fingers with your left palm facing the direction of the ball.

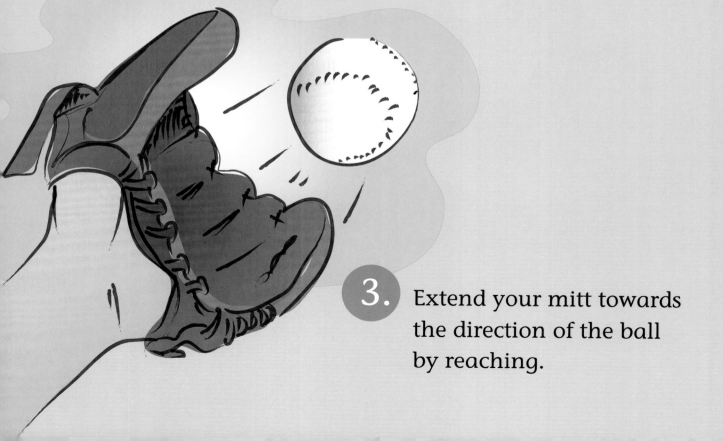

3. Extend your mitt towards the direction of the ball by reaching.

4. When the ball enters your mitt squeeze it shut and cover it with your right hand.

5. Try to catch the ball with the pocket of the mitt and not the palm of your hand.

It may help to practice catching by having a partner toss the ball underhand to you until you are comfortable.

Glossary

base: The square plate at each of the four points of a baseball diamond: first base, second base, third base, and home plate. A runner must touch all bases in order to score a run.

batter: The player for the offense who stands at home plate with a bat and tries to hit the ball.

offense: The team taking turns at bat. They are trying to hit the ball and score runs.

defense: The team playing out in the field. They are trying to prevent the other team from scoring runs.

run: A point scored by a player for the offense who has touched all four bases without being called out.

home run: Scored when a batter hits the ball and runs around all four bases without stopping.

out: An out happens in two main ways:

1. When a runner tries to run to a base and a player from the other team tags her with the ball or holds the ball while stepping on the base.

2. When a batter strikes out or hits a ball into the air that is caught by the other team.

About the Author

Shelly Boyum-Breen grew up playing sports in her neighborhood with friends, her brothers and on her school teams. She found that the life-long benefits of sports for girls were so important that she needed to write this series and inspire girls across the world to play. Shelly resides in Minnesota with her spouse, has two adult daughters and continues to play sports and be active.

About the Illustrator

After designing books and working as a creative director in publishing, Marieka made the leap to become a children's book illustrator. Now with over 30 picture books in print, she loves creating artwork that engages and educates young readers. Marieka always aims to draw an environment where all children can see themselves, as well as the big wonderful world around them.

More action packed books in this Series:

- **Shelly Bean the Sports Queen Skates at the Hockey Rink**

- **Shelly Bean the Sports Queen Plays a Game of Catch**

- **Shelly Bean the Sports Queen Plays Basketball**

    And many more...